Invisible Army

Sarah Mcnee

ISBN: 978-93-6354-032-3

First Edition: 2025
Rs. 200/-

Cyberwit.net
HIG 45 Kaushambi Kunj, Kalindipuram
Allahabad - 211011 (U.P.) India
http://www.cyberwit.net
Tel: +(91) 9415091004
E-mail: info@cyberwit.net

Printed at Repro India Limited.

Introduction

My poetry consists of a mixture of my own experiences and thoughts

Some I've written from an empathetic point of view touching on other people's experiences

I connect with my intuition and imagination to create scenarios based on words I was given as a writing exercise during the 2020 pandemic

Some of my poetry is written in code based on the name meanings of people in my life

I hope my words can help heal and teach as and when possible

Blessings to you and your loved ones

Through the darkest times and experiences some of the most beautiful works of art are birthed

Chakra cleansing

I hold my crystal
my left hand it lights up
I pass it to you
your whole body lights up
every muscle it touches it relaxes and heals you
I know you feel it because my heart it feels you
your body lit up with a silver outline
the light it turns red at the base of your spine
eliminates pain and energy spare
every tiny molecule every single hair
orange from red your pelvis sacral portal
time scaled body strong spirit immortal
up the light rises from orange to yellow
active solar plexus sunshine says hello
renewing emotions from yellow to green
the heart chakra charged now active and clean
moving up from the heart to the throat bright blue
vocally healing ..confident you
voice box clear and freedom of speech using it wisely to comfort and teach
next up the third eye indigo bright
processing visions lucid dreaming at night
indigo light to manifest
all hopes and wishes of only the best
from indigo to violet chakra seven
the temple door and gateway to heaven
protected and cleansed with bright purple light
activated crown all balanced sleep tight

Anthem

To identify with me
A song must simply be
Indeed with life experienced flaws Performed by magical beings of course
Must contain variety
Mass Expression of empathy
Soft and delicate symphony
Guided through eternity
With a dash of history
Glorious waves of magical bells
Natural sea sounds made with sea shells
Shamanic drums and singing bowls
Didgeridoo like totem poles
Animal noises and sounds of trees
Chirping birds and bumble bees
Haunting sounds to give you the chills
Hypnotic trance beats
Adrenaline thrills
A children's choir
Street rappers too
At the centre of my very own anthem is You

Beautiful Queen

Traveling French Canadian Beautiful Queen
Sparkling eyes angelic serene
For every Queen must have a crown
God blessed her
A platinum garland was sent to her
God's Purest most stunning jewel was lent to her
Breath-taking beauty too precious for earth
Stefany crowned from birth
Melissa sweet as the honey in her name
Honey bee she gives strength to her Queen
Manon, Melissa heartbroken team
Together they are healing
Take strength from believing
From heaven she shines the Queens precious crown
Replaced with a halo he sent angels down
Divine intervention blessed us dear friend
Stefany shines with you this life's not the end

Shadow

Out the front door and into the street
Traffic in distance The atmosphere speaks
Swinging steel logo so rusty it creeks
Ghost train railway rumbling sky
Wobbling and stumbling drunk passes by
Parallel bus stop the bench bare and yellow
Then out of nowhere the silhouette fellow
Like an angel he keeps me company
Accidental art right there in front of me
Illusionary protector still kitten did god send?
I like you regardless my shadow feline friend

Culture defined

Combination of ideas birth of the creative mind
Expressed through Arts
Representation of traditions
Mix of all mankind
Historical revolutionary excitement of all who break through
In the heart of the now. Relived by me.. expressed by You
A picture painted and expressed through performance
Examples of blessings through strength and endurance
Lessons results built on improvements
Past and present creative peace movements
When poverty tragedy leads to solidarity
It leaves a mark on the community
Inspires creativity
And through struggles found unity
And for those who are closed suppressed and blind
The Art of the creative is culture defined

3am

It’s 3am the witches hour
Lights are out but within there’s power
Never ending supplies of light
Emergency stash but not in sight
Not the artificial blinding type
Natural fuelled like a star filled night
Layered pollution thick clouds cover sky
Fooling the fools even covers their eyes
So whilst the sleeping are deep in to dreaming
Bewildered the witches from inside are beaming
Some can not channel they hate how they’re feeling
Congested conscience they wake up to screaming
Bless them this hour Bless all of them
The cloud covered folk at 3am

Humble free man

Free man heroic family title
A story written light years before he was conceived
A man of his word He stands by his wife
And through pain came the light this man received
He grieved
He grieved for his boy
His beautiful Son named worthy of praise
His troubled son so handsome
Once a child so pure
He suffers no more
Besides him God like lady Joan
Together they mourn
Through pain a heroic play writer was born
Angels sent birds to drop seeds in the ground
A spot where the sun shone wild flowers He found
They spread and they blossomed
Brought butterflies and bees
More flowers grew
Beneath skies were angels flew
Miracle garden keeper this is for you
Heroic story teller
May your dreams come true

Celebration of demons

Tonight's the night have you not heard
Toffee apples have been prepared
Wonderful pumpkin carving creations
Creepy decor and illuminations

Monsters and zombies roam the streets
Pointed hats webbed hands and feet
Awakened corpses arise from their tombs
Black cats and witches fly past on brooms

Sightings of mummy's and trails of blood
Are taking over the neighbourhood
Nightmare scenes strange characters from books
Chopped off hands replaced with hooks
Teenage rebels causing commotion
Demonic mix of witches potion
Untrusted treats with bags of tricks
Spiders and slugs a wizards mix
Treading carefully not to be cursed
Of course it's October 31st

The band with five hands

Little Jimmy Bailey a Liverpool lad
Lived with his brothers and drunken dad
His mother walked out she couldn't cope
Never even left them a bar of soap
So little Jimmy with the dirty face
Wore shoes with holes and only one lace
Quick witted and fast good with his hands
Made a guitar from a box and Rubber bands
Oh he loved a sing song young Jimmy did
He wrote songs in his head since he was a kid
As he got older and opened his eyes
His songs kept on coming and words got more wise
All the practicing with elastic bands
Made Jimmy a star with his voice and his hands
He started to busk and saved up for some strings
A second hand keyboard and musical things
He got really good and formed a small band
Franny the drummer and Steve with one hand
Every night they would jam together
Got a few gigs and rocked up in leather
They called them selves the band with five hands
They were booked up 'til Christmas had no time for plans
Before they knew it they were touring the sky's
Living the dream with stars in their eyes
Numerous hits they were top of the charts
Back at their digs for beer pizza darts
Although there job was far from boring
The band agreed to split after touring
They were grateful enough for their glamorous life

All that was missing was kids and a wife
They set off together back to Scouse land
With all of their riches they made from the band
They boarded the plane with memories of magic
I'm sorry to say the ending is tragic
The plane lost a wing before it could land
A one winged aircraft and a five handed band
They sunk in the ocean never to be seen
That was the end of young jimmy's dream

Corkscrew of sin

Were are you now my love
My sorrow my pain
For love is pain
Sharper than blades
Explosive bombs destructive grenades
A mix of all emotions
Heat from the sun waves of the oceans
Heart and soul bottled as potions
Nothing but a cork keeping them in
Oh fragile glass bottle oh cork screw of sin
Remain untouched no pressure applied
Non aggravated carefully captured inside
To speak is to unscrew irreversible True
To break open is to free
Not now am I ready for now I shall be
Just bee
To sting would mean death
Blessed for a breath
Honey is my living
Not present for taking all for the giving
Forgiving
No control addicted my love my drug
Foggy crazy time consuming
Day dreaming mutual assuming
Withering heights to me or I'm Juliet found my Romeo
Can i rewrite the ending?
The title I would give is tragedy mending
Just thoughts I am sending
All else is neglected you are my obsession

These words confession
For you have my heart
You have from the start
For I am inside the bottle of glass
You see through me
See light through me
Dismissing my message
Now free me Love me unscrew me
Then screw me
Spell cast back to the druids
Be cleansed in my fluids
Be high highest tower
Magnetic power
Everlasting non repelling magnetic force
No need for force
Magic surrounds me oh winged horned horse
Long horn so empowered
Drench thee be showered
Unforgettable unamusable mess
Sacred God blessable bless
Combinable souls
Living up to thy roles
Fictional deceit
Invisible pair
Invisible discrete
Worship thy feet
For you more purpose than walk
Moistened lips more purpose than talk

The power of giving

What is life without a fight
Without rights
Do we live to fight for our rights
When is it right to fight
To write about fighting for rights in this life
This short life
Before you know it it's over
It's done
Your day has gone
The only rights you got now are your last
Last rights
Memories
They're flashing before you
Visions of all that you seen and who saw you
Your brothers your sisters your parents
They adore you
They went before You They struggled in battles
Before you
They did it for you
And they let you know
Did you understand it? No?
Not until it was there time to go
Time to let go
Only then did you see
Eyes wide open now
You're hoping now
Youl be coping now
Minus their presence
Now just the essence

No physical presence
It's dull nothing to show
No one to show
You what way to go
This way that way ..right or left
How long left
No one knows
That's the point I'm making
Give more than you're taking
We all need waking
Open your eyes
Realise
Don't let them fool u get wise
This life is a gift be free
What you can't change let be
Explore the sea
Hug a tree
These things are free
Cry show tears
Eliminate fears
These days are yours. Your years
Why you fighting the wrong fight
Wasting energy
Demolish with light ..the light you were given
So bright
You hold it tight
Release it let go it won't run out
Like time
Enjoy your time ...spend time
Don't rush. Take your time
Make love last
Days go fast
Live today like it's your last

You are a gift ..life is for living
The secret of life is the Power of giving
Forgiving
The power of giving is living
Peace

To send or not to send

Words were spinning in my head
Voices opinions the lot
By the time I'd figured what to say
I'd already forgot
The ice was spinning round the glass
Dissolving into the gin
Internally planning this move until I could no longer keep it in
A text I'd been wanting to send for a while
I'd write it and then I'd delete it
I changed it like a million times
Erased and then I'd repeat it
Over thinking room spinning
You guessed it
I text it
Did I send it?
Nar i couldn't ...no credit
I Just left it

Solar storm

Solar storm awakening july
Happened to hit the earth on birthday number seven of this child of mine
July 19th of course one and nine
According to numerology this means accomplished one plus nine is ten
Chapter closed
A new one starts again
Complete you are my special boy
Completely blessed am I
The solar storm it cleansed you
Blasted away any negative impact on your first precious seven years
Released your heart of sadness and burnt away your fears
My child you are a healing ball of adorable mischief
Senses highly attuned ever adapting to your surroundings
My beautiful innocent kind little boy
And you are musical
Simply beautiful
For you I am grateful
Your presence delightful
Blessed views you are insightful
Protected by Archangel Michael
Your faith is pure
Your thoughts are deep
You know things
In all light white feather things
Your intent to comfort sounds to me just like when God sings
You make my tears fall

Sometimes I cause it all
You've got my back always and I won't let you fall
You are my world and more
My boys right by my side
Right there I've got it all
They'd never let me fall
Oh bless us solar storm

Telepathy

Telepathy
According to the English dictionary
Is described as
“Supposedly”
Perceived by me is suggestive of conspiracy
When actually
Overlooked it seems that we
Communicate this naturally
Chemistry
Science and mythology
Injected to society
Almost projecting not in so many words subliminally
Less such topic touched on systematically
The subliminal tactical form of trickery
Down played discreetly
It’s saying move on to the next word
There’s nothing else to see
Sore subject apparently
Distracting away from the brilliance of telepathy
Like I said it’s trickery
And the method used for such mind trick
Is the powerful method of Telepathy
Obviously
Does that make sense ?
Or just to me ?
Drop me a telepathic text I’d like to know your thoughts
Actually

London

South on the map
Google maps app
A city were royalty base
Big Ben the clock
10 downing Street mob
Fast living then this is your place
The rarest of sounds
They got underground
They busk to the beat of the trains
Night foxes roam
The streets are now home
Upon primrose hill daisy chains
Rappers and chanters
Camden stall banters
A plate full the hungry for fame
The theatre's the restaurants
Quaint breakfast croissants
The all seeing big London eye
Red busses Black taxis
Big toy shop hamleys
Heathrow the airport lets fly
Pearly buttons on blouses
Much overpriced house's
They all do the great lambeth walk
Crisis on coaches
One man blamed for roaches
People who rhyme when they talk
The culture the history
Masonic mystery

The rats plague and fire was no joke
The bridge that once burned here
Lessons to learn here
Oh so that's why they call it the smoke?

My magical pets

Dark night black four legged creature
Sparkling stars your eyes such feature
Elegantly ruthless hunter by nature
Sharp claws and teeth
Trusted structure
Ears they point to the sky
Triangles
Short straight hair
No tangles
Perfectionism to perfection Grooming essential
Deep and moving thoughts
Undiscovered potential
You chose me
My black cat
My jet black stunning cat
Yellow/Green eyed portal
Nine lives
Almost immortal
Like me
Communication telepathy
Accompanied Vocal intimacy
And then there's your daughter
Shiny black miniature
Innocent she has
A protector mature
Wisest black totem life Because of lucky's impurity Scarlet is pure

Arthur

Strong as a bear
You guide me
Never write alone as I write
There's a presence besides me
Helping me to be the best to express emotions deep inside me
I didn't believe in myself the way I do now
I didn't know you then as well as I do now
Your girls they miss you
I let them know you are around
The signs you leave me
The king you are crowned
Me I am the lucky one
You chose me to pass your knowledge on
For years I wanted to write
I scribbled and jotted and then overnight
The words started flowing
With my new guide my spirit is glowing
Iv written this book
Il publish it soon
With your Divine guidance
And whole of the moon

Relapse

Broken in pieces
Metaphorically
Literally shattered
My soul feels bruised and battered
Years of lost trust finally found over almost a year
Gained in time but lost again through fear
Warned stay clear
All things toxic drugs and beer
Disappointment unspoken but visual
Her eyes are sad she looks miserable
She blames her self they all do
The handful of people who got me through
But back again soul is black again iv been untrue
I lied again to my self lied to you
Guilty mess out of the blue
Unfortunate relapse
Choose one of three maps
Choices..death..gloom or success
I choose success
To clean up this mess
I'm an addict it's my lifelong illness I don't
Look Ill
This disease deadly no stranger to kill
High or low no moderate never still
Oh higher power guide me by the hour
For they who love me are torn
Renew me offer me reborn

Sebastian

I value you
A soul protected
Guard you like a delicate rose petal
Words do not describe your existence
You give me reason
Every decision I make
Is with your best interests
You are my life
You are deep my son
You are vulnerable
You may not know it
Nor may others not
But it's in your name
Sebastian
My clear cut high carat diamond
Unbreakable like a diamond
April Spring Diamond
Because of you I am rich
You are the start of my creativity
I see sparkles and rays of natural colour shine from you
My Son I adore you
Proud is a master understatement
But words do not exist to me
To project what you mean to me
God Sent you here
I am grateful
I am blessed
My Son My life

Invisible army

to be controlled
like really controlled
no exception the effort
my life you hold
I yes Me
as it stands
to be confined in the palms of your hands
My talents and gifts
do they not matter
as you clench your fists
my soul does shatter
so why did you send me down
I ask?
to disguise my beauty
behind this mask
a delicate flower
the Art god mastered
hardened cemented
pebble dashed and plastered
a life time spent
with jokers and fools
in faith in the distance is
you with your tools
patience
is what has got me to now
my patience you've tested
but I'm still here still patient somehow
the silent fighter amongst
the robots

they think I know little
but I know lots
an emotionless army
dismissing my intelligence
disguised and staged
crowd pleasing elegance
The fact I'm labelled but saying
this now
proves I'm ahead of your system
allow
for in this racing brain full of knowledge
my truth is from me
I don't need your college
I can't act out a script written
for many
just to add to the tax payers penny
unique mechanisms my
unique brain
my golden silence
you label insane
so I stand waiting my demolition
to break down the walls
of the politician
discrimination contradictions you push us aside
medicating numbing
many have died
not I
to speak your language
to generalize
neuro-typical robots
then there's us sent from the sky's.
blessed with solutions and
answers unheard

freedom on way
for every caged bird
to you a parrot just feathers
and beak
deny him his wings
now he does speak
intelligent creature with
miraculous wings
incarcerated but talks
and sings
I feel you parrot
beautiful bright
caged up and lonely
deprivation of flight
get ready the birds
cages will rattle
freedom joined forces
our spiritual battle
the silence will break
come bring your tools
ready so strong
now who's the fools
darkness get ready
freedom in flight
unfortunate robots
defeated by light
darkness fooled no one
but the dark for too long
you caged us you thought you
had won but ..wrong
Artificial lights and
processed dinners
Real verses fake and

guess who the Winners
the tables are turning
magical soon
it takes just one candle to
light a dark room
I fear nothing.. no fear
silent fighter
darkest weakness
love makes us brighter

Put a label on it

Young mum with a stroller
A double rum and cola
Take away that edginess
Nervous twitching
Wait
I know her
There's the hooded lady
Smoking looking hazy
Magic yeah she's crazy
Wait
wise woman
Don't go there
Off she goes now spending
Glamour life pretending
Don't decline still pending
This hoarding never ending
Freeze
The build up to the big fight
Training hard on each night
Night time until daylight
Roller-coaster sit tight
Prepare
The Real battle starts
When the show is over
Welcome to bipolar
Label
Not to be consumed
But the product can consume
Cling to the recipient
Not that it's significant
Bipolar makes him different

Signature

I can hear the traffic in the distance
And some far away clock
Swoosh goes the early cars out to work
Phone vibrations drown out tick tock tick tock
He is not here with me ..the sofa feels
Spacious and empty
Oh does his hard labour resent me
He would rather be laid here with me
I'd rather he stayed here with me
His face lights up when he sees me
True love He says that he needs me
Drinks his coffee we kiss then he leaves me
So dull when he leaves me
I need him he needs me
No man has an Aura like his
Musical dressed in hi-viz
T-shirt tan messy curly
I wish you never left so early
It is all to give us a future of course
One day my signature will end just like yours

Food

Food with roots and leaves
Eating plants and trees
I see this as life on a plate
I see meat as death on a plate

Shona

Gracious and merciful she's 22
Fairest adult child
Fresh northern dew
Planter of seeds the special one grew

Purest of petals silk white her mane
Bright yellow white green young daisy chain
Heavy her heart beauty her power
Nourished in sun soils
Her flourishing flower
Articulate humour Yorkshire scouse jock
If foundations aren't solid
Girl I'll be your rock

Jane

Gracious as her title
God Blessed the earth with this noble warrior by name
Like oxygen to survive she is vital
Unique lady unlike any other
For Jane we are blessed Bright mother
Her heart dances and sings
Fine cut like a diamond
As golden as her rings
This lady is flamboyant as true as her beauty
She oozes style
Eyes sparkling like stars I see her soul in her smile
She cares and loves
To some she is misunderstood
One daughter one praiseworthy son
Love in their blood
Well spoken and funny simply priceless
Forever grateful I am for you jane
Without you life would be lifeless

Armour of God

You know that if we prayed for each other
If we tried to do whats right
Lets say we didn't Hate one another
Nor overcome with pride
Freeing elevating our brothers
Getting clean from the inside
Sisters celebrating gracious mothers
That attitude has died
Dead and buried

We try to fix what was never broken
Creating cracks and then we mask them

Insane poet who's words aren't spoken
Confusion fuled questions but too scared to ask them
Just ask them
Actually..hmmm

Better we know less
The system is hopeless
All follow the goat ?yes
Distraction from own mess
Expression through style dress
Try being homeless
Or pray for them God bless

Protection our father
He gave us a sword
God's sacred armour

Protection ignored
Sword of the spirit
Oh righteous breastplate
Helmet salvation
Bright shield of faith
Truthful strong belt breathe in and release
Walk now protected oh gospel of peace

Perish

Daily battles
Hourly battles
Life is a battle a constant battle
We win some we lose
Give up if we choose
From evergreen
Never to be seen
Over taken by concrete
Trees down. Over crowded
We build and we build
Yet shortage of houses
The gluttonous folk tongue money and power
Conscience they lack as we drop by the hour
Care not do they for the bills we can't pay
We are to them necessitous vermin
Surviving on their scraps
Many do not survive
Like rats we are poisoned
Devoured alive
If the earth is our mother one assumes we are her babies
Forget the if's forget the maybe's
Our mothers milk has been contaminated
Nutrition to venom
Father we need you almighty heavenly Father
A mothers love is one to cherish
Yet we perish

Little wonder

I wonder if you hear me,I wonder what you think
I wonder if you're liking the things I eat and drink
I wonder how you're sleeping is everything okay
I wonder what new limbs you have and how much you've grown today
Are you a boy or a girl? I have a feeling you're a girl
Does your hair grow straight or does it have a curl
What colour will your eyes be
How much will you weigh
Did you like the music I was listening to today?
What's your favourite sound is it mummy when she talks
Or is it noises from the outside world when mummy goes for walks
I love it when you move and the way it makes me feel
You're reminding me you are there.. letting me know that you are real
I'm holding the responsibility to take care of my health
Now i've got you to think of ..it's no longer just myself
The day I see your little face and hold your tiny hand
Will be the happiest day of my life and it wasn't even planned

Paradise moon

New moon bringing peace bringing light
New moon bring healing
Devine powers this night
For our brother has been taken away too soon
Bless him new moon

Bless them his family the children blessed niece
Our brother will guide us with heavenly peace
This pain we feel
This heartache its real
To heal we must feel
To become strong
We fall and rise
We learn
We teach we grow until we meet again
In paradise
For to know him is to be blessed
Beautiful brother now you may rest

Honour my choice

So I've thought out this letter for so long as the times have
changed my words have too everything changes but my mind this
windowless prison permanent guard oh shadowed screw
Understand ..This was carefully planned
I did consider all options fooling myself. Knowing other options
weren't an option
Constantly fighting and am tired I'm locked away double pad
locked and it's cold in here nothing you could have done
I don't belong here
I' m sorry I tried I tried and tried now I'm tired
Don't blame yourself please I know this will hurt but one day I
hope you find peace knowing this was my choice
Please honour my decision
Remember my voice
Cherish your life as I struggled to live mine
Every day I tried to mask my truth my heart it hurts it hurts so
deep my head feels broken
Its unbearable
Irreparable
Just know that this was my path
Please live your life if not for you for me
By doing that you set me free
And I will guide you
These are my only wishes
Your acceptance your forgiveness
I took with me my beautiful memories
Until we meet again please please
Know that when you read this I will not be suffering
No more pain

Amy

They let you down sweet child
27 as you predicted
Your heart was broken lady
Neglected fooled addicted
They could never get your soul though
You guarded it so proudly
Displayed it in your words
As you sang your heart out loudly
You created history sweet angel
Unfinished unnurtured child
Your Nurtured soul we cradle
Soul cleansed with tears you cried
Today you still inspire as you changed dynamics of music
You teach me.. I teach my lover
Your gift your style I use it
Soul sister permission you gave me
When they ask who inspires your art
I tell them of course it is Amy
Melodic the strings in your heart
And when he struggles with words my lover your lyrics I'll hand them
Troubled.. now queen of the skies and forever your throne
Queen of Camden

The only cure

Oh beloved
Flying high
God may have taken you back early to those you left behind
What was yours on earth your precious connections
To each other " we" each other were just stories and experiences solemnly yours although you would share so precisely the beauty you embraced
In each individual
It was like you connected us through your own sentiment whilst playing your songs
Every conversation savoured and enjoyed
You actually used your time wisely
You touched the hearts of many
You spoke so carefully but with passion and the deepest of empathy
Admired soul brother ..an Angel
Not because you left for paradise
But because you came from paradise
The people you chose experienced paradise
Earthly burdens and pressure released
You came to protect
Eternal protector with us you left your gift
Over time you are healing us
Almost like you never left
We feel you and know that you're feeling us
Angel
Big tall giant angelic being
Wore glasses for seeing
From another era another plaine

So commonly used beloved name
You taught us Love is the only cure for pain
That is instilled now
That can't be reversed
Positive change
Love heals pain
The only Cure

Square chalice

Oh chalice you hold the purest
Disguised your milky grey complexion
Hints of sky blue golden sun
Creative nature rippling on reflection
Clear waters run
Carrying with it the sun
Collecting soil gathering particles of leaf and tree residue
Slowing the flow of the mineral spring
Giving the porous chalice time to absorb
It never seems to overflow
The temperature doesn't alter
Oh chalice you are to the squirrels a bath
Cleansing feeding the ground
Nourishment supply to the grass the trees
Pool for the dogs in summer to play
Square sharp cornered chalice
Miniature spa
So nurtured ..they dress you
A display of beauty perfection
Secret but unhidden
On display and always a treat to the virgin spring vision
If one is to visit oh square water bed
Make wishes untouched chalice for she cleanses the dead
The historical underworld where human temple shells retire
Bring life to the living ..she inspires with hand carved stonemason words
Feel inspired Just admire
Rest ancient bodies
Cleansed souls do not tire

Plot 2 the allotment

Down at the bottom of the allotment
Just in front of the tall trees
Is a magical little world
Of butterflies flowers and bees
A green house a shed a Japanese arch
Vegetables nurtured and seeds sown in march
Broad beans and beetroot and straw-berries too
Recycled decor some old and some new
Life size scarecrow hand made fish pond
Hand crafted bird bath creative and beyond
Stained glass window from the rose pub
Terracotta chimney pots
Ceramic bathtub
Windows from a skip top
And the 7a bus stop
Berries pears and flowers
The list goes on for hours
Beautiful foot paths to avoid getting muddy
But best of all
My Dad and Buddy

Telepathy

Telepathy
According to the English dictionary
Is described with words
Ie."Supposedly"
An Adverb leaking doubt with suggestive hints.. conspiracy
When actually
Overlooked it seems that we
Communicate this naturally
Chemistry
Science and mythology
Grey clouded
Injected into society
Almost projecting ..not in so many words subliminally
Less such topic touched on systematically
The subliminal tactical form of trickery
Discreetly
Its saying move on to the next word
There's nothing else to see
Sore subject apparently
Distracting away from the brilliance of telepathy
Like I said it's trickery
And the method used in the dictionaries
To fool the likes of you and me
Telepathic method Telepathy
Ironically

Vogue

Silk wraps baseball caps
Cotton bow ties on wedding hats
Vintage buttons on modern jackets
Handbags designed like crisp packets
Fishnet tights and lycra cling on
Printed t-shirts Jeans with bling on
Rara skirts with vivviene shirts
Tight mini dresses for all you flirts
Over the knee boots
Boots with studs on
Jogging bottoms and tops hoods on
Pattern socks odd socks if you're feeling silly
Trainer socks bed socks
Favourite socks are frilly
Tight fitted playsuits
Prefer baggy lounge suits
Designer heels Shoes with with wheels
Art is fashion whatever your style
However you dress don't forget your smile

40

Families
Separated
Nerves are shattered
Understated
Loved ones lost
Devastated
Scared to hug or go outside
Minds lost
Suicide
Coughs and sneezes
Catch it
Politicians chat shit
Absolute bull shit
Rules no news and that's it
Child killers knife crime
Husband kills his wife time
Don't assume the men are fine
Drinking smoking one more line
Depression breeding lazy
Darker world it's crazy
Can't sleep he's wide awake
Its light outside for God's sake
How much can his body take
The lock down thing it taught me
Life is my own story
Chapters lines and words
And someday it will flash before me
And to my friends who never reached 40
This ones for you
Rest in paradise

Capital

It's Paris I'm cycling a beret on head
Bonjor over cobbles
A basket of bread
Soyez notre invité.. Soyez notre invité
je pense que tu connais la suite
Was French now I'm German
Forgive Me
God Bless Me
Oh look its Berlin
Mein Rhythmus ist Techno, aber nur solange ich hier bin
Washington the Whitehouse Madrid and Millan
Then top of the morning its Dublin
Ooh Guinness
Gwon gwon gwon until Finnish
Oh Finish its Finland
Hello Helsinki
Henna rakastan sinua sielusisar
A part of my heart is a piece of you there
Capital City's with status
Titles
Decent enough to represent Its country
Fit for presidents and royalty and power
So the Capital of England what is it ?obviously the answer to the question is E

Proximity

When one radiates such toxic electricity
Subtle imbalances are apparent to me
Bright but unnatural brightness
Synthetic
Almost comparing sunshine to a sunbed
There is no comparison
Toxic radiation in the form of false U V
Unlike the sunshine vitamin D
Skin so thin and pure
Rose petal
Forced tough and prickling heat
Like a nettle
Invisible daggers spores and virus
Ghostly sound waves burn through the wireless
It makes sense to distance one's energy
But depending on ones frequency
Like attracts like regardless
Proximity
Toxicity
One can prevent this toxic attraction
Take action

Magnanimous

For in this life we suffer
Sufferings are inevitable
Not all are unpreventable
Many are preventable
Lesser of the minds so cautious
Risk assessment minds of the wise
The oldest souls
Those who tread in care
With care
360 visionary eyes in the back of one's head
Many eyes like a peacock
Nothing goes unseen
Awake even when sleeping
Clarity expressing ones dream
No matter the level of consciousness
Leaking the consciousness of the unconscious
We can not control the minds nor the actions of another
When they wrong us that be a lesson
Forever learning
Forever teaching
For one to remain magnanimous is truly a gift

Celestial

The stars I hold as electric beams run through me
Vibrating I'm moving a zillion miles an hour the moons just let on like he knew me
Present
Blow back the kisses the sun has just blew me
Love
From the planets so truly
Recharge put celestial through me
Give
I share out what you have given to me
Times ten it returns right back to me
To enable one to keep it..one must give it away
It's simple really and so overlooked
Our spirits join forces and there is no going back
Just forward with moments of silence for reflection
Privacy intimacy
Constant protection
Spirit connection
As one

Certified

Gliding through the life force element
Water you carry me
The tears of joy when the day comes I hear you say "marry me"
Water in dreams represents emotion
For each tear shed each year contributes to the ocean
The seas and rivers ponds and lakes falls and streams
Are all of emotional significance if appearing in dreams
Recognise these symbols take Lessons see signs
Take blessings from these testing times
Understanding is key to survival in some cases not necessary
The cat murderer ...curiosity
Acceptance and forgiveness show Gratitude
Stepping aside. Edging away ..Measuring distance... Latitude
No control swinging mood
Tell them straight "nar it's rude"
Be the eater not the food
You'll be appreciated more when you've died
Birth and death are the only achievements guaranteed to be certified
Additionally if you are willing to walk the extra mile
If you do ..my advice to you ..whatever you do
M
Do it in style
Your style
Smile

Yolanda

Sweet little lady in pineapple socks
Amethyst pendant with matching dreadlocks
As she bottled spring water cathedral hydration
Spoke of soul food ..nutrition meditation
Suppressed uniqueness a thing of the past
"My name is Yolanda" she said when I asked
I looked up the meaning purple it means
Purple her aura with earth browns and green
Violet earth angel at the Anglican tap
Hope we meet again and continue our chat

Counting sheep

Rest time at bed time is not always the best time
When I can't sleep.. they say to count sheep
But my sheep don't help me they keep me awake
My eyes scared to close incase my soul they take
I know it's an exercise to rest one's mind
My sheep in my head are not very kind
I try to count them jump as they say
Some of them run in the opposite way
Some are too small and jump and clash heads
They're cut and they're bleeding and white wool turns red
It's sad and frustrating and I'm unable to help
Instead of the baa sound these sheep scream and yelp
The big ones are mean and they ram with their horns
They kill all the weak ones and hurt the new borns
Then after hours of those graphic scenes
I slip in to sleep land for horrific dreams
I'm scared and I'm lonely and can not get out
And no sound will come out as I try to shout
I'm fighting and losing my body inactive
I feel hopeless and paranoid and so unattractive
Bed times surrounded with dark dreads and fears
I dont always remember but wake saddened in tears
Other times I'm drifting feels like I'm watched
Night sweats and terrors oh when will this stop
Sleep time for others for granted they take
The best thing bout sleep time is when I awake

Maybe

The thought of you alone, only a spirit no physical mechanisms to communicate although I suppose you thought that through?
Maybe you were born knowing and it was your purpose a secret between God and you
Maybe you tried so hard to ignore the pain
Scared of your thoughts fears of insane
Did you know something that no-one else did
Had this planned since you were a kid ?
You knew you were loved surely
You loved back and expanded it purely
Clearly suffering you generously gave
Like you were on a mission to save
You forgot about you and your own mental health
You forgotten to save yourself
You did so much for others
Your family your brothers
They miss you like mad you know
Maybe their comfort is that you chose to go
Or was this you crying for help and went wrong
Listening for clues song after song
Maybe just Maybe there's so much more to it
Left questions unanswered like "why did he do it"
Your special authentic soul in paradise has landed
Maybe you could let them know you're not stranded
Be free my friend spread your wings
Somewhere up there an angel he sings

The chosen grain of sand

At the bottom of the sea sits a perfectly symmetrical hinged oyster shell
Lived in water and land
Inside is a grain of sand
That chosen grain the special one
In to the gap in the shell he has gone
At first it is lonely and dark cant get out
But he's safe from the monsters of the sea no doubt
This tiny grain with sharpened points
Indulges and grows as the shell anoints
He tumbles and roles in the empty shell structure
Gaining some layers and gradual sculpture
After suffering storms and daily sea beatings
Other tiny grains make their short but sweet greetings
In time he strengthens to a bashing he's immune
Finds it hard to roll in an ever shrinking room
The cracks get bigger as the grain takes shape
Institutionalized but ready to escape
Exposed
Triple A graded
Welded
Set and hallmarked
Give us a twirl
That grain of sand is now a Pearl

Soul mates

Traditional local vacations
Blackpool illuminations
Lighting up a town
Making dark nights bright
To lift spirits when feeling down
Dark so dark unable to see
Then you come along on a lighting spree
Sparks from you fly off to me
I now shine like a Christmas tree
Twin flame duo side by side
Glowing outward flames never ending
Together bright souls darkness mending
Shining brightest infinite soul mate
Brought together to illuminate

Mersey pride

Born in a city in the north west of the map
A city with the friendliest football divide
A place of magic on Merseyside
I was raised here
Praised here
Put down here
Gave birth here
Forever loved here
Forever in love with here
Home of the Beatles
Cathedrals with steeples
The finest of peoples
Culture and art were ever you look
A helping hand if ever you're stuck
Our city of the best
We are the eggs of the liver birds nest
We speak unique with Liverpool passion
Scouse boutique our Liverpool fashion
Artists and singers story tellers
Glamorous ladies and the best lookin fellas
We fight for our rights the genuine folk
Wonderful northern not short of a joke
Here the people give when they dont have a lot
I'm a scouser ...not biased ..but a patriot

Magic moon tree

Moon Angel we talk through the moon
Sun rise at dawn settle at noon
Evening comes and darkness is ours
Oh blissful darkness you give us the stars
Night streams and moon beams
Glistening waters
Reflecting on lessons the night Time
Has taught us.
The blessings it brought us
Still many lessons and magic to come
Magical teachers the stars moon and sun
Yes there were hard times and there will be more
Water fall tears melting from frozen core
But with these tears are invisible seeds
Intentions of new life as this soul bleeds
Pain of the invisible sort from within
Heaviness guilt malice jealously sin
Let it go
Let your tears fall
Let go of it all
And eventually you will see
The invisible tear seeds have become a tree
Watch it ripen let nature be
Evergreen leaves and bottomless fruit
Blossoming flowers and expansive root
And this tree doesn't die its
Forever strengthening
Home to the birds
Branch ever lengthening

Full moon portal of magical light
Expand all seedlings this magical night
Bless all my loved ones and help them to see
Make with their sadness a magic moon tree

The passing of the storm

We survived all weather's all seasons each year
We are combined forces so bright we eliminate fear
I keep you near you keep me near
The reunion of souls so overwhelming so precious blinding
..piercing familiar brand new
My soul stopped searching and connected to you
Perfect fit the key turned so effortlessly
Locked tight combination code 11.11
Mixed eras one soul in sync transformation 7
Fragile immortal creatively fertile
My heart melts when you smile
It's true we are twin flames
We've no time for their games
With spiritual guidance the holiest form
Our hands locked in lockdown
No longer a storm

Blessed dove

White oh so pure rare delight
Asking for signs snow white doves close in flight
Beauty and love serenity and peace
I wish in your life from my heart doves release

Balloon

Yesterday I was a helium filled balloon all sassy and metallic.
Outstanding
Full bright and shiny
High but grounded
Celebrating life
Then out of nowhere to my despair
Deflated as I was popped with a sharp pin
Now just a empty lifeless saggy bag
Thanks for that

Monumental

Happy alone although not physically alone
Just two repellent magnets incompatible forces
Fighting to pull closer but no efforts could make the scientifically impossible...possible
Not in those circumstances at that time
The facts were just the facts
Unsigned unwritten laws bound by unspoken pacts
Small print unread but thankfully unsigned
Well technically
Just not systematically
The benefit of this should have meant free will
The God given right to walk away from dangerous poison
The spiritual binding oh child 'at birth I grant you this prison
Weapon I name thee
I sharpen you proudly
Attack or defend for me
You work both so brilliantly
Now hush just sit silently
Further away from me
Don't let the neighbour's see
They're all round the bend you see
This mother's love is an endless river of sadness
Unsure unappreciated unpretty badness
The insecurities and kindness combined it confuses me
We shout and He bruises me
Their hearts beat
In the rhythm of the kitchen clock
It needs new batteries
That reminds me.. my children need recharging

I do too
2017 along came you
Electric.. broken burnt out
Magnetically compatible with my force
No doubt
Blessed with how it turned out
Monumental transformation
For every second I am blessed
Lawfully bound side by side
True love at it's very best
The finest

Our Nan

I love you with all my heart
So much to say ..were should i start
My special glass clown I look and i see
A lifetime of love that was given to me
A happy house
Food and drink always dozens
My nan she would sing to me and my cousins
Up those white steps what a magical house
Fresh crusty bread and hot bowls of scouse
"Come to the nan queen" that's what she'd say
Her spirit lives on and gets stronger each day.
What a woman my nan was.. for her i am forever blessed
Back with our Grandad both simply The best
Never goodbye as you continue to guide us
And whatever we go through you will be besides us
With your strength ill dry my tears
And celebrate your life of 96 years
I love you so much nan go and be free
You live on forever in the others and me

Mummy

A woman who I can only describe as my world my universe
My brightest light ..my tonic ..my backbone my nurse
Even in black she has more colours than a rainbow
Brighter than the moonlight the sunshine she makes the rain go
When I'm told that I'm magic and I'm gifted
It's coz of her she keeps me uplifted
I have been so low
But never solo
She is the light that attracts light
She's the stars in the night
She's beautiful makes heads turn
So hot she'll give u sunburn
She's one of them who suits all hats
All styles of glasses
All hair do's
Looks classy in her house coat
Her uniform
My favourite. .her pinny
My mum in a pinny makes my Heart warm
I want to squeeze her forever
She makes me feel safe and she makes me feel special...she keeps me going
Gives me power she keeps me glowing
Her life is dedicated to us and I can't put into words how much I love my mum
Iv plenty of words ..only worthy are some
You can do absolutely anything if you put your mind to it
And if the storm comes we battle through it
She taught me that..

She can party all night but still does the dishes
Up fresh out to work...giving love and granting wishes
She's nanny Mandy to Sebastian Austin
Mum to many and Jodie and me
Most of all
We have a ball
We are a family of light and we are proper boss
We love with all our hearts and do magic stuff
I love my mum she's always there
When I grow up
Il be just like her

Graveyard Tim

Once again at cathedral water
Myself, a red balloon, my friend and her daughter
From nowhere it seemed a pug dog named petal
Drank from the pool natural man made tap nettle
Not far behind was a man with a cap on
He spoke of dead rats near the step we were sat on
He pondered on reasons and spiritual meaning
Birth charts, statistics totem rat readings
old church ullet road ways
He mentioned a dance class I think he said Tuesdays
I don't remember many details I just felt he was trying to mend
His heart has been broken
Healing I send
In time he will mend
I gave him crystals
The dance class of course I said count me in
I asked "what's your name"?
He replied with "I'm Tim"

Hayley over the road

A meadow of hay she is free
Creative and laid back is she
Up and out early
Boisterous but girly
Two years younger than me
Boss at karate
Quiet but chatty
Dimples and freckles so sweet
Cheeky and small
A queen at football
Apparently she's got flat feet
For years wouldn't see her
I'd call her she'd be there
I was scared I was losing my way
She brought rescue remedy
Slept in my bed with me
Even when she didn't want to stay
Miniature coke cans
She's got one in each hand
She would buy 10p crisps by the load
30 years on
Iv still met no one
Like Hayley over the road

This Little light of mine

Its mid 70s the families of liverpool they struggle
Born babies the products of scandal and trouble
A woman in love at the time with a drinker
Mentality destructive disturbed man dark thinker
He cared not a lot for his sons wife or health
Inside relives torture he's suffered himself
The wife didn't know this she cant understand
This was not what the vows read when gave her left hand
For better for worse though is what she vowed
You may kiss the bride now the priest said out loud
Fell pregnant. Late teens so marriage a must
Her father a catholic so sinful is lust
Time it went by as the cracks just got deeper
Violent. She left him but he wants to keep her
Her babies she loves them ..armed robberies clothed them
occupation her husband all types of crime
No income to feed when her husband serves time
Mentally unwell she shows no affection
Drugs drink abuse and now she has been sectioned
Her eldest a soldier got murdered at war
Lonely her youngest has no one no more
He grows up all messed up
A daughter now blessed up
He still cuts his chest up
To bleed out his pain
His daughter the product of unhinged insane
To save his daughter his friends tried to save him
Understanding non judging time they all gave him
Medical emotional support he was given

Progressive reflective his darkness was hidden
His cousin found hanging and father found dead
"You still got me" his daughter she said
She bandaged her dad up and wiped up his tears
This was her birthday of 12 painful years
His struggling best friend who helped raise his daughter
When he could not feed her..his friend would support her
Tragedy struck and spread to next level
We had nurtured a soul long claimed by the DEVIL

Passenger

North Liverpool taxi ride
It was a clear.. autumn... day outside
But everyone was unaware
Of this special day on Merseyside
I spoke to the driver in the cab
He asked what I thought about the stag
The stag I asked what do you mean
It's all over the news haven't you seen?
There has been sightings in the North of the city
An animal rare so sacred so pretty
Snow White fur ..antlers such power
Was roaming the streets of Bootle this hour
This mythical mystical animal so rare
Will only appear with a message to share
He symbolises the God's on earth
He comes to reverse the darkness curse
He represents heavenly angelic dimensions
Pureness with magical healing intentions
What a blessing he chose this city
To transform bad and ugly. To good and pretty
To surface our struggles and guide us to light
To join our front line in this spiritual fight
The enemy the system of whom darkness rule
Lacking conscience and empathy one language being cruel
What did they do with this mythological stranger?
They shot him dead
The police shot him dead like he was a danger
I won't ever forget that taxi ride
RIP WHITE STAG

www.ingramcontent.com/pod-product-compliance
Lightning Source LLC
LaVergne TN
LVHW040952150826
845672LV00002B/655

* 9 7 8 9 3 6 3 5 4 0 3 2 3 *